Roister Doister Publishing

Only in the Dark

by Matthew Clift

WWW.ROISTERDOISTER.COM

About the Author

Matthew Clift

Matthew has worked as an actor, a director, an education officer in regional theatre and a college lecturer.

His debut play *Recidivists* was seen at the 2011 British Final of One Act Plays and was subsequently published by the
Drama Association of Wales.

Other plays written includes an adaptation of Chekhov's Swan Song entitled *The Final Act of Henry Gladstone* and *Funny Ha Ha!* written with Becky Cann.

Only in the Dark
by Matthew Clift

First published in Great Britain in 2016 by
Roister Doister Publishing
The Swan Theatre
The Moors
Worcester
WR1 3ED
info@roisterdoister.com
www.roisterdoister.com

ISBN: 978-0-9932619-7-8

CHARACTERS

Vic
Anyone.

Ernie
Anyone.

Gnod
Anyone.

SETTING
Unknown/Anywhere

Only in the Dark was first performed by Whole Hog Productions at the Unicorn Theatre, Abingdon in June 2014 as part of the Oxfordshire Drama Network Festival of One Act Plays and went onto to be performed at the Corn Exchange Drama Festival, Wallingford in July 2014.

CAST

Vic	Darren Little
Ernie	Maxwell Sly
Gnod	Dominic Bray

PRODUCTION TEAM

Director	Matthew Clift

It was subsequently revived by Whole Hog Productions in August 2015, staged in a Double Bill with Jane Shepard's 'Nine', performed at the Alma Tavern Theatre, Bristol.

CAST

Vic	Michael Sly
Ernie	Maxwell Sly
Gnod	Grace Scott

PRODUCTION TEAM

Director	Maxwell Sly

Only in the Dark won the following awards.

Selected for Gala Performance Evening at 2014 Oxfordshire Drama Network Festival of One Act Plays.

Best Production at the 2014 Corn Exchange Drama Festival, Wallingford.

Only in the Dark

A One Act Play

by Matthew Clift

ONLY IN THE DARK

The stage is in darkness. There is an eerie silence. We become aware of people on stage, although we do not see them. Out of the darkness comes a voice

Vic
Ernie? Ernie? Ern? Err? Eeeeeeee?

Ernie
I'm here

Vic
Then why didn't you answer?

Ernie
Because I enjoy hearing you shouting out my name then, all of a sudden, forgetting it!

Vic
I know your name *(Pause)* Ernie.

Ernie
How many years have you known me? And you still have to think for my name.

Vic
Alright smarty pants, what's my name?

Ernie
Your name is irrelevant.

Vic
I'm irrelevant?

Ernie
No, I didn't say that. I was merely implying that in the many decades that we have been in each other's company you always struggle to remember my name. Recalling your given forename was not the topic of discussion

Vic
You don't remember, do you?

Ernie
Are you deaf?

Vic
Dead?

Ernie
Seems to prove my point!

Vic
Eh?

Ernie
No, not eh! It's Ernie!

Silence

Vic
When is it coming then?

Ernie
You ask me this all the time.

Vic
I know!

Ernie
How long have we been here?

Vic
Blimey! Now, that is a question.

Ernie
Well, yes obviously it's a question.

Vic
One that I would struggle to answer.

Ernie
Let's just say that in the HUGE amount of time we have been here you ask that question on a daily basis usually, more than once and every time my answer is always the same.

Vic
Which is?

Ernie
I don't know!

Pause.

Vic
Be nice if you gave a different answer once in a while.

Ernie
What do you want me to say?

Vic
Just something…different

Ernie
What would be the point?

Vic
Make things a bit more…interesting.

Ernie
No it doesn't. I might give you a different answer but it would mean exactly the same thing wouldn't it? The fact is I don't know when the light is coming! I wish I did, but I don't!

Vic
You mentioned the *(whispers)* light!

Ernie
And?

Vic
You should never, ever mention it because if you keep wearing out its name it won't ever come!

Ernie
Oh god! *(Pause)* I know what you're going to say next.

Vic
Do you?

Ernie
Yes.

Vic
How do you know?

Ernie
Because you are transparent.

Vic
But you if you can't see me how do you know I'm transparent?

Ernie
Not literally transparent…oh never mind! *(Pause)* I meant you are going to ask if we can use our daily ration.

Vic
I might not be asking that?

Ernie
Yes you are.

Vic
I'm not.

Ernie
You are

Vic
I'm not

Silence.

Vic
So…can we…

Ernie
YES!

A small flash light comes on that shines on Ernie & Vic's features. They stare out to the audience, silent for a moment.

Vic
Explain to me again why we can't use the ration for anymore than two minutes a day?

Ernie
You're doing it again

Vic
Doing what again?

Ernie
Asking me questions that you already know the answer to

Vic
Am I?

Ernie
Yes

Vic
It's nice and warm isn't it?

Ernie
It is, yes.

Pause.

Turn it off now.

Pause.

Turn it off now

Vic
But it's so nice

Ernie
We agreed, one minute now then one minute later

Vic
Yes, but…

Ernie
TURN IT OFF!

Ernie tries to grab the torch off Vic. They struggle for a moment. The light goes off.

Ernie
See, told you times up. We can't use it later now!

Vic
Can't we?

Ernie
You know we can't!

Vic
Why not?

There is the sound of a swift punch and a yelp!

Ernie
I didn't want to do that! You forced my arm!

Vic
You forced you're arm into my face!

Ernie
I lightly slapped you!

Vic
You hit me!

Ernie
Well, you were asking for it! And I didn't really hit you I...

Vic
YOU...HIT... ME!

Pause.

Ernie
Ok, I apologize I shouldn't have slapped...

Vic
Hit!

Ernie
Hit you! But we survive by this delicate balance of order that we have imposed on our existence. We can't keep going round in circles like this, we have to maintain order and maybe one day the *(whispers)* Light will come. But it won't arrive if we continue to question, squabble and fight. Remember, the prophecy 'it only comes to those who wait a beam of light from heaven's gate'. Patience is what's needed now!

Vic
I know all that, but what if the prophecy is wrong? What if, in order for it to come, you have to rediscover the way to exist?

Ernie
But that doesn't mean we have to change our daily rituals. That's not guaranteed to shake him out of his lethargy!

Vic
Lechery?

Ernie
Why do I bother?

Vic
Good question!

Ernie
That wasn't a question it was a statement.

Vic
Sounded like a question to me.

There is a silence. Then Ernie lets out a full throated scream! It lasts a few moments.

Vic
What did you do that for?

Ernie
Isn't it obvious?

Vic
No.

Ernie
Look, I'm not...

Suddenly, from the back of the stage, a faint light appears.

Vic
Look!

Ernie
How can I look its pitch black isn't it!

Vic
No... Look!

The light becomes clearer to the audience. A voice accompanies it.

Voice
Is this the way? Is this the way? I need to know...

He is cut off by Vic.

Vic
We are over here!

Ernie
Shhh! Quiet, he might not be the one

Vic
Do you see anyone else with a light?

Ernie
Well, no but that doesn't mean...

Before Ernie can finish, Vic dashes over to the light and it illuminates his face. The light is from a bulb. For the first time we see the face of the person carrying the bulb. This is Gnod.

Vic
We have waited decades for you to illuminate the way!

Ernie
Vic, wait!

Vic
No, Ernie this is it! Tell us why you bring the light?

Gnod looks at him puzzled for a moment.

Gnod
This bulb has been attached to me forever. I take it here, I take it there I never rest. It burns my hand, it scorches my face. I search for the string to tie the light. Is this the way? Do you have the string?

Vic
String?

Ernie joins them.

Ernie
What string are you talking about?

Gnod
He who has the string releases my burden. The light will be shared, my journey will be over

Vic and Ernie look at each other. Ernie takes Vic to one side.

Ernie
This is a crucial moment. He does indeed seem to have the light but the prophecy says nothing of string?

Vic
Maybe it's a test?

Ernie
A test?

Vic
Yes. If we can provide him with string then he might share the light with us

Ernie
We have no string!

There is a sudden moan from Gnod. He is holding the bulb up into the air. This illuminates the space above him. The audience sees a light bulb fitting hanging from the ceiling.

Gnod
It is over! I have found the keepers of the string! How long has this been here?

Vic
That? Oh that's nothing it's been there forever

Ernie grabs Vic.

Ernie
(In a violent whisper.) Tell him nothing!

Vic
Why?

Ernie
Why? What do you mean why? We have existed together all this time and now this 'stranger' appears and our whole lives are turned upside down.

Vic
But we have been waiting for the light and now it's here you want to turn it away!

Ernie
I didn't say I wanted to turn it away I just think we need to be…careful.

Vic
Careful? We've always been careful, I don't want to be careful, I want the light and if it means letting him use some pointless piece of string that has dangled above us, serving no purpose then so be it!

Vic breaks away from Ernie. He goes over to Gnod who has been staring up at the ceiling. Vic kneels down before him.

Vic
Oh master! You are the prophecy you may use our string so that you can share the light with us all!

Ernie sighs at this and puts his head in his hands. Gnod climbs onto Vic's shoulders and he lifts him up. Gnod attaches the bulb to the light fitting. There is a moment of darkness and then a sudden burst of light as the stage is bathed in white light. Vic lowers Gnod down.

Vic
What now oh prophet of the light?

Gnod
This is all. My burden is over.

Gnod sits down and closes his eyes, fully content. Vic watches him do this and then does the same. Ernie watches them. Vic motions for Ernie to join them. After a while Ernie sits beside them but has his legs crossed and looks unsure! The light begins to fade. We hear the sound of 'Own Personal Jesus' by Depeche Mode. Lights up. Vic & Gnod are just staring up at the bulb, in a trance. Ernie stands between them looking at the ground, Lights out. Lights come up to reveal Vic & Gnod moving around the bulb in some kind of ceremonial dance. Ernie is stood still staring out to the audience, lights out. Lights come back up and we see Gnod & Vic stood frozen and smiling, Ernie watches them for a while then stands next to them and starts to smile, small at first then big, bold and as beaming as the other two, lights fade. Lights up on Vic, Ernie & Gnod, Vic is pointing out to the audience in 'catalogue' pose. Ernie is knelt down smiling; Gnod has his hands on his hips looking majestic, Lights fade. Lights up Gnod who is wearing a 'Kiss Me Quick' hat on, Vic eats some candy floss and Ernie wears a ridiculously coloured afro wig, lights fade. Lights up and all three are sat in different parts of the audience looking up at the light bulb, lights fade. Lights up on all three still stood in a line. Each is doing the classic 'see no evil, hear no evil, speak no evil' monkey pose, lights fade. Lights up on Gnod asleep on the floor, almost sunbathing under the light. Vic is sat smiling, Ernie looks up at light. He looks down, he seems puzzled.

Ernie
Do you think this is all there is?

Vic
What?
Ernie
Do you think this is all there is?

Vic
I certainly hope so!

Ernie
But is it all we hoped for?

Vic
And more!

Ernie
Yes, but…

Vic
There are no buts! We waited for the light, it came, and we finally start to live that's all I know. There's no need for any questions

Ernie
Hmm… It's just

Vic
What?

Ernie
Aren't you getting a little, well…?

Vic
Well, what?

Pause.

Ernie
Bored?

Silence.

Vic
Bored? BORED? Are you serious? Since it arrived everything has been wonderful.

Ernie
I will admit that our routine has been changed and, on the surface, seems to be better.

Vic
That's what's great about it, there is no routine!

Ernie
But we lived by that routine for years. We got by.

Vic
You always moaned about it! You were always screaming and hitting me!

Ernie
I know, I know! But in some strange ways don't you wish we had that order, that stability. Being able to do things on a whim begins as an adventure but as you go on you realize that in gaining something, something else has been taken away.

Pause.

Vic
I have no idea what you are talking about?

Ernie
Look, the light has been…nice but…

Vic
Nice? NICE? It has been our saviour! I get up every day and I don't sigh anymore I smile, I sing, I leap! All because I know that I don't know what is going to happen. I'm no longer waiting

Ernie
But aren't you still 'waiting it's just a different kind of waiting?

Vic
I don't understand?

Ernie
What I mean is before the light came we knew what we were waiting for; we were secure in the knowledge that we had a definite goal. But, now we don't have a purpose! We simply drift, like paper boats on a river, never knowing if there is a waterfall to come. Don't you see, we are still waiting!

Vic
No, I don't see. All I know is I am happier with the way things are now.

Ernie
"But doth not the appetite alter? A man loves the meat in his youth that he cannot endure in his age".

Vic
Who said that?

Ernie
I don't know I'm just trying to make you understand that although we may have changed one state of affairs for another state of affairs, they are essentially, in essence the same thing!

Vic
You are trying to ruin this for me aren't you? Ever since I have known you've had this overwhelming desire to control things and push me around. But, no more! I'm free Ernie, FREE! I'm not going back to the first state of affairs, no way Jose!

Ernie
See, it has affected you more than you know. You forgot my name! You called me Jose. I have no Spanish origins

Vic
Oranges?

Ernie
No…

Vic

I'm not falling into that trap! You deliberately made me mishear you just so you could have the balance of power back!

Ernie

How can I make you mishear things?

Vic

You did! I know you're name is not Jose, it is just an expression

Ernie

An expression?

Vic

Yes, an expression that Gnod taught me

Ernie

I see, we are getting down to the truth of things now!

Vic

What's that supposed to mean?

Ernie

Do decades in the dark together mean nothing to you? We shared the darkness, we waited and waited, together and now you want to forget that friendship!

Vic

You can't exactly call it a friendship! We shouted and argued all the time! We just survived together!

Ernie

But that's something isn't it? Survival is what it's all about! We were the only two left!

Vic

Don't misunderstand me Ernie I appreciate that there was someone there with me during the darkness but now we have the light. The light has changed everything! I shouldn't have to rely on you now and you shouldn't have to rely on me. We are free!

Ernie

It's just this…Gnod person. I'm not sure I trust him.

Vic

You should make an effort and speak to him more. You were happy for a while.

Ernie

Yes, I know but now there is something else…

Vic
You have no way of enjoying yourself have you? Speak to him, get to know him.

Ernie pauses. He looks at Gnod still laid down on the floor. He motions to Vic to move away, which he does. Ernie sits next to Gnod. There is a silence, eventually Ernie speaks.

Ernie
So…this light really is…bright

Ernie winces at his poor attempt at conversation.

What I mean is the light is very pleasing and is enabling us to have a really… jolly time

Ernie stops speaking. Gnod slowly sits up and faces Ernie.

Gnod
I know you. I know your plan. If you continue the light will be returned.

He lies back down. Ernie sits frozen for a moment. He slowly sits up and moves over to Vic.

Ernie
It is as I thought! He is not the real light bearer. Do you know what he said to me? He said he knew my plan and the light would be returned!

Vic
You are totally paranoid!

Ernie
Just because people are talking about me it does not make me paranoid!

Vic
He was talking to you, not about you and I'm sure he said nothing of the kind!

Ernie
He did, I swear!

Vic
I'm sorry, I simply don't believe you

Ernie
Oh really? You know something, you've changed!

Vic
Yes, I have and I like me now! I don't have to take orders from you. I was a caterpillar but I have come out of my cocoon, I AM A BUTTERFLY! I HAVE WINGS, I CAN FLY!

There is a silence after Vic's outburst.

Ernie, I think its best that we don't speak for a while. You go over there.

Ernie moves only slightly away from Vic.

Vic
No, over there!

Vic turns his back on him, Ernie is stunned by this turn of events. He walks slowly away from Vic and Gnod. He stares into space. There is a prolonged silence. After awhile Ernie looks up at the light. He looks down at Gnod who still lies motionless, he looks back at Vic who has now also laid out on the floor, his hands behind his back, eyes closed and with a grin on his face. Ernie looks back up to the light he suddenly leaps into the air and pushes the light. It swings violently backwards and forwards, Gnod and Vic sit up. There is a smashing sound and then darkness. Silence.

Vic
What's happened? Ernie, what have you done?

Ernie
I have restored order!

Vic
No! You've sent us backwards.

Gnod
Nothing left. All is gone, I have to start again. You didn't listen to me! The light has gone, it has been returned. It is time for me to leave.

Vic
Wait! Don't leave us what are we going to do?

We hear Gnod slowly leaving. Silence.

Ernie! I'm going to kill you!

Vic lets out a scream. We hear the sound of a full on fight! After awhile there is another silence. Suddenly, the torch light is seen sweeping around the theatre. It comes to rest on Vic and Ernie's faces.

Vic
Ernie? Ernie? Ern? Err? Eeeeeeee?

Ernie
I'm here

The torch flickers off their faces then darkness. We hear the sound of Johnny Cash's version of Depeche Mode's 'Own Personal Jesus'.

End

Roister Doister Publishing

Founded in 2013 Roister Doister Publishing was created to rethink theatrical publishing, give a quality start to new writers and a more 'in touch' approach to established writers. Roister Doister Publishing endeavours to make writing, publishing, and producing theatre as easy as possible for both professionals and amateurs.

HOW DOES ROISTER DOISTER PUBLISHING DIFFER FROM OTHER PUBLISHERS?

Upfront and Up-to-date Information

All the information you need to make a decision regarding a play will be at your disposal from the moment you look at our website. License fees, availability, and permissions will all be on the play's Roister Doister page enabling you to make the right decision for your company.

Quality Control

Unlike other online 'publishers' we will not just blindly accept any script for 'publication'. We will give each script submitted to us careful consideration and advice before we release it to the public, even in our New Work section.

Investment in our Playwrights

All great theatre begins with a great play. We will invest in our writer's work and creative property by not only providing a store front for their scripts but also a professional profile for the writer where they can build their public awareness.

If you enjoyed this script please ask your local library to stock our titles.

www.ingramcontent.com/pod-product-compliance
Lightning Source LLC
Chambersburg PA
CBHW071806020426
42331CB00008B/2413